**Karton
Kuties**

Karton Kuties

Written and Illustrated by
H. Wayne Edwards

The Naylor Company
Book Publishers of the Southwest
San Antonio, Texas

Copyright ©, 1971 by THE NAYLOR COMPANY

This book or parts thereof may not be reproduced without written permission of the publisher except for customary privileges extended to the press and other reviewing agencies.

Library of Congress Catalog Card No. 70-139592

ALL RIGHTS RESERVED

Printed in the United States of America

ISBN 0-8111-0390-0

Karton Kuties

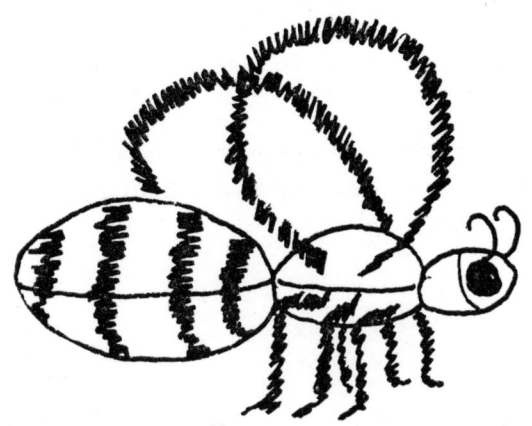

Octopus

Materials needed: 2 egg cups from colored egg carton; 2 large colored beads for the eyes; 8 pieces of colored pipe cleaners three inches long; black felt pen; straight pins

1. The octopus is one of the most simple objects to make. Put two of the egg cups together with glue to make the body of the octopus; pin until dry.

2. Cut eight pieces of desired color of pipe cleaners three inches long for the legs. Insert the end of each pipe cleaner in the base of the egg cup an equal distance from each other.

3. Use the black felt pen to make a round circle for the mouth.

4. Pin round colored beads above the mouth and on either side for the eyes. Finish eyes and eyebrows with black felt pen.

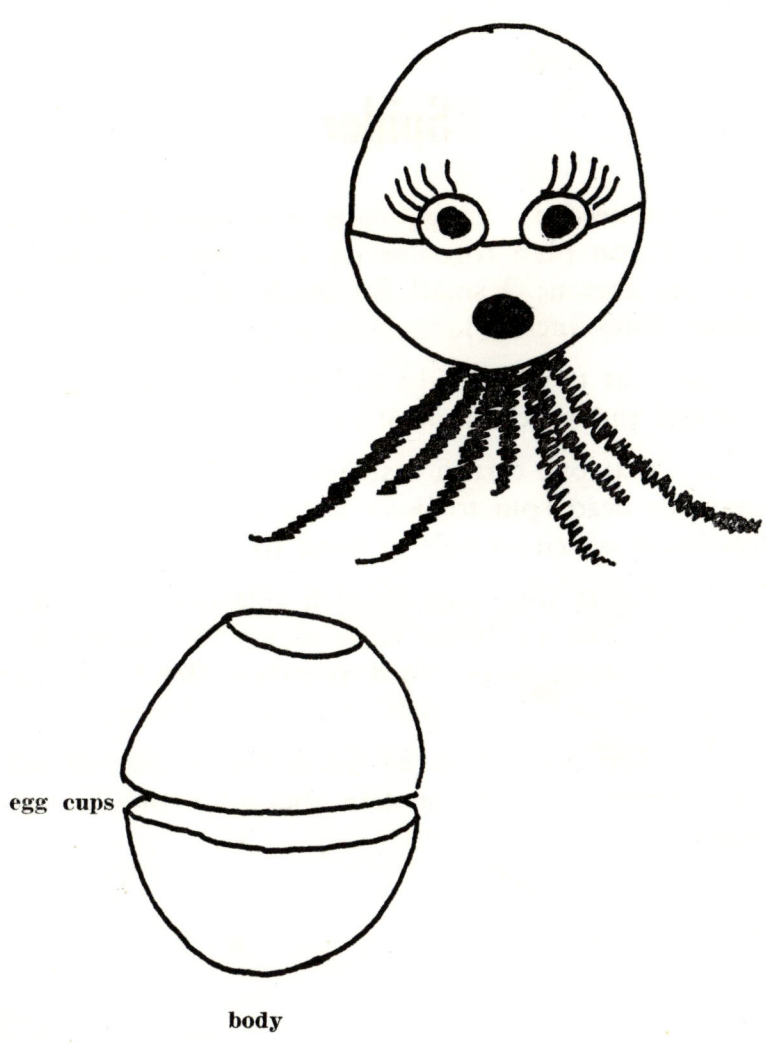

egg cups

body

(2) beads
eyes

(8) green pipe cleaners
legs

Spider

Materials needed: 2 egg cups, the desired color or white if you plan to color it; 1 of the lid fasteners from the carton; 2 small flat beads; 8 pieces of pipe cleaner three inches long

1. Cut two egg cups to form the circular body; glue and pin together until dry.

2. Cut one carton fastener and glue to body to make the head; pin to body until dry. After drying, glue beads on either side of head for eyes.

3. Insert four legs on each side made of three-inch pipe cleaners. Insert these along the median line where the cups were glued together. Bend the end of each leg about one-half inch from the end.

4. The body may be colored with colored felt pens, tempera paint, or left the color of the egg carton.

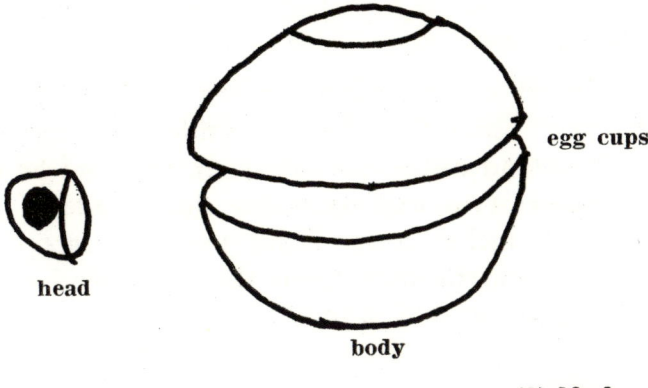

head

body

egg cups

eyes
(2) beads

(8) black
pipe cleaners

legs

Turtle

Materials needed: 2 egg cups from a green egg carton, or white if you wish to paint; 1 lid fastener; 4 pieces of green pipe cleaner two inches long; black and brown felt pens; straight pins

    1. Cut the two egg cups, one a fraction larger. Place the large one on top and glue, then pin to dry.

    2. Paint the top shell with a brown felt pen and outline the scales with a black felt pen.

    3. Cut one lid fastener for the head, glue to the shell, pin and let dry. Color black dots on either side for the eyes.

    4. Insert a small pointed sliver of the styrofoam for the tail. Glue this directly under the top shell and let it extend out about one inch. Pin and let dry.

    5. Insert two legs on either side, made of pipe cleaners two inches long. Bend pipe cleaners down about three-fourths inch from the top. Bend out at the bottom so it will stand.

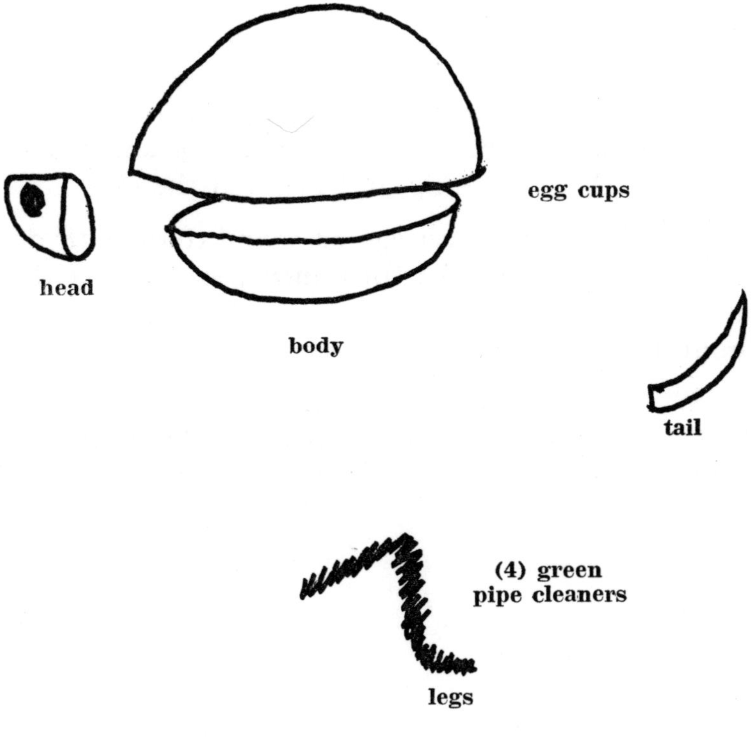

head

egg cups

body

tail

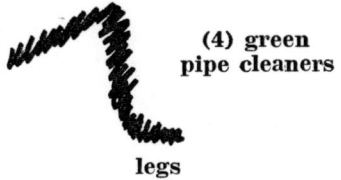
(4) green pipe cleaners

legs

Beetle or Lady Bug

Materials needed: 4 egg cups any desired color; black felt pen; a round toothpick; 6 pieces of green or brown pipe cleaners three inches in length; 2 one-inch pieces of floral wire

    1. Cut two egg cups and make them as large as possible; this will form the body. Glue and pin together. Then cut two more egg cups a little smaller and glue and pin together to make the head.

    2. Take the smaller cups and with the black felt pen paint a black dot on either side of the head for the eyes. Then make a line for the mouth. Insert the one-inch pieces of floral wire to make the antennae on the head. Place these up and between the eyes.

    3. Take the larger egg cups and color with dots or as desired. Insert the three-inch pipe cleaners three on each side to make the legs. Bend each leg down about three-fourths inch from the end.

    4. Take the round toothpick and insert between the large and small egg cups that have been glued together, then glue to hold body and head together.

egg cups

head

body

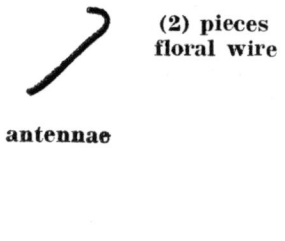

(2) pieces floral wire

antennae

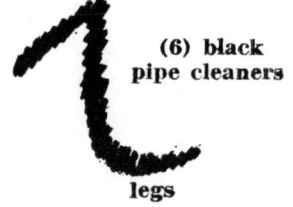

(6) black pipe cleaners

legs

Bee

Materials needed: 4 egg cups from a yellow or white egg carton; black and yellow felt pens; 2 round toothpicks; 8 pieces of yellow or white pipe cleaners; 2 short pieces of floral wire; 2 of the lid fasteners from the cartons

1. Cut two egg cups and make them as large as possible; this will form the abdomen. Glue together and let dry. Color black stripes around the abdomen.

2. Cut two more egg cups a little smaller; glue and pin together to make the thorax.

3. Cut the two lid fasteners and glue them together to make the head. Paint two large dots on either side of the head with a black felt pen, for the eyes.

4. Take one round toothpick and insert between the large and small cups that have been glued together, then insert the other toothpick between the small cups and lid fasteners.

5. Insert three pieces of pipe cleaners on each side of the thorax. Bend each leg down about three-fourths of an inch from the end.

6. Curve two pieces of a pipe cleaner to make the wings. Insert on each side of the thorax.

7. Insert the one-inch piece of floral wire to make the antennae on the head. Place these up and between the eyes.

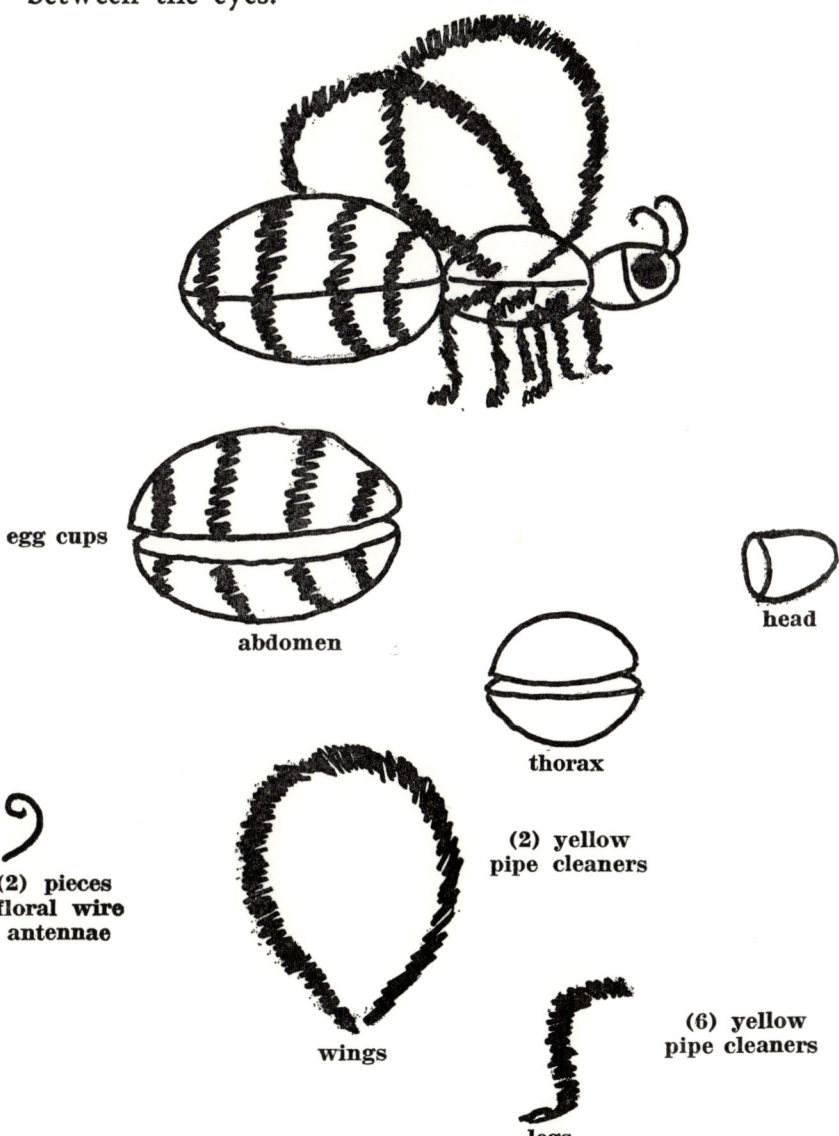

egg cups
abdomen
head
thorax
(2) yellow pipe cleaners
(2) pieces floral wire antennae
wings
(6) yellow pipe cleaners
legs

Worm

Materials needed: 10 yellow or green egg cups; 1 lid fastener; 8 pieces of yellow or green pipe cleaners three inches in length; black felt pen; 2 pieces green light weight floral wire about four inches long; 4 round toothpicks

1. Cut eight of the egg cups as large as possible to make the worm segments. Glue two together to make the four worm segments; pin and dry.

2. Cut two egg cups smaller to form the head. Glue together, pin and let dry.

3. Make two large black circles on the head for the eyes with black felt pen. Insert floral wire above the eyes and curl for antennae.

4. Insert one piece of three-inch pipe cleaner on either side of each segment to form the legs. Bend about one inch from the end.

5. Insert round toothpicks between each segment and head, then glue.

6. Cut fastener tip and glue to the last segment to make tail.

head

egg cups

body

lid fastener

tail

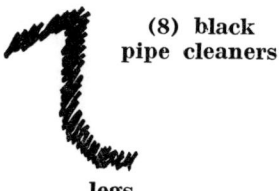
(8) black pipe cleaners

legs

Fish

Materials needed: 2 egg cups from a green, yellow, pink or white carton; the lid of the carton for the top fin and tail fins; 2 flat beads for the eyes; black felt pen; glue; straight pins

1. Cut two egg cups and make them as large as possible; this will form the body. Glue the cups together, then pin and let dry.

2. Cut the top fin and tail fin from the flat part of the carton lid. Shape it to fit the body. Glue and let dry.

3. Cut side fins from side of egg cup. Cut to fit sides of body. Let the side fin flair out at the bottom to help make a stand for the fish. Glue and let dry.

4. Glue and pin beads for the eyes.

5. Mark the mouth with a felt pen; also, mark the fins.

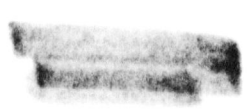
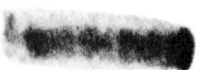

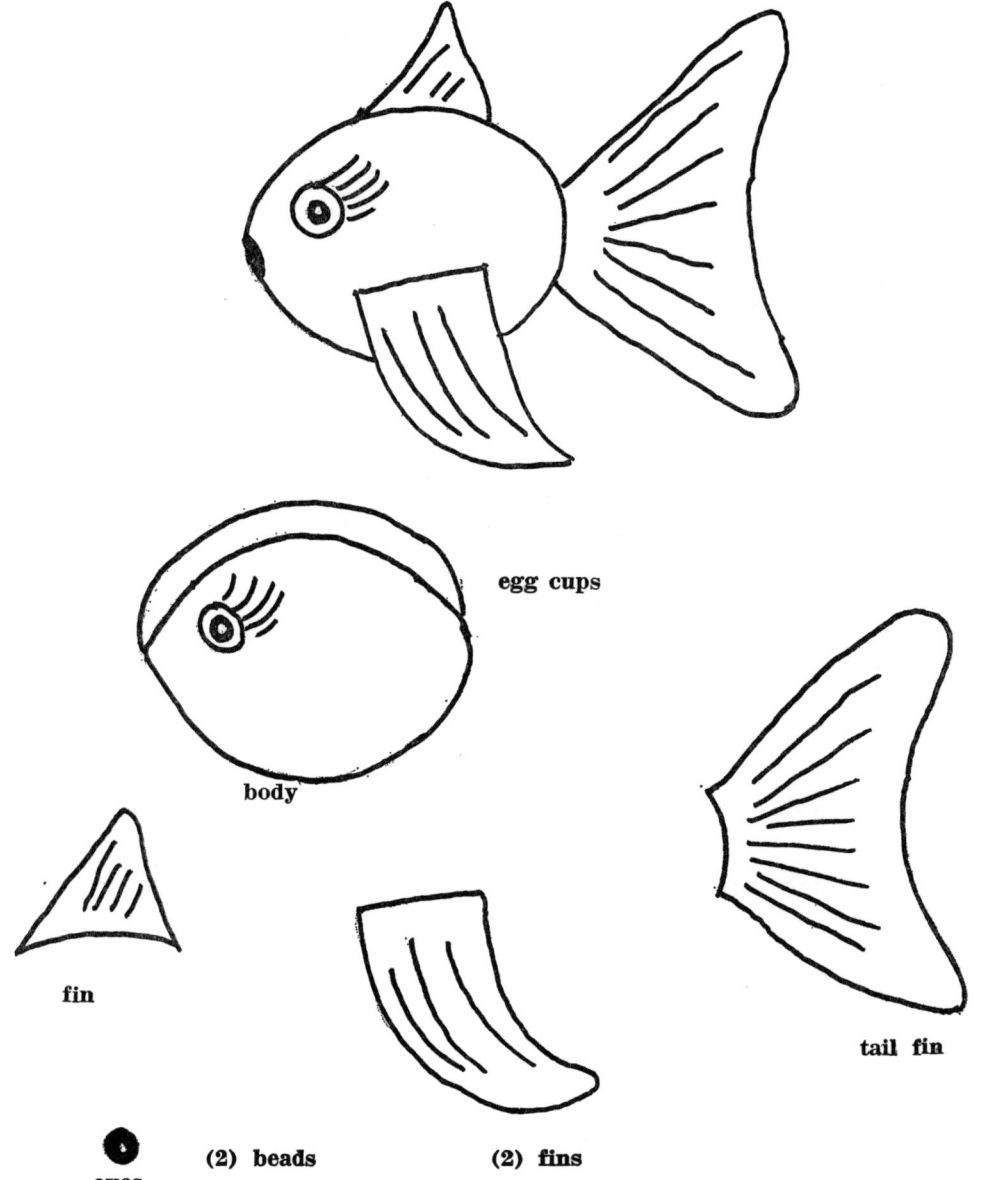

Duck

Materials needed: 4 egg cups from a yellow or white egg carton; the lid of the carton for the feet; 2 sides of an egg cup for the wings; 2 of the peaked portions of the lid for the tail and beak; 1 feather; black and orange felt pens

1. Cut two of the egg cups and make them as large as possible; this will form the body. Cut two of the egg cups smaller; this will form the head. Glue the cups together, then pin to dry.

2. Glue the head and body together and let them dry.

3. Cut the feet from the lid; glue to body and let dry.

4. Cut the wings from the side of egg cups; glue in place and let dry.

5. Cut the beak and tail from the peaked portions of the lid; cut to fit the head and body; glue in place and let dry.

6. Put feather on top of head; draw in the eyes with black felt pen, and color the beak with orange felt pen.

Woodpecker

Materials needed: 4 egg cups from a yellow or white egg carton; the lid of the carton for the feet; 2 sides of an egg cup for the wings; 1 of the peaked portions of the lid for the tail; 1 red feather; 2 small pieces of styrofoam for the beak; a black felt pen; straight pins

    1. Cut two of the egg cups and make them as large as possible; this will form the body. Cut two of the egg cups smaller; this will form the head. Glue the cups together, then pin to dry.

    2. Glue the head and body together and let them dry.

    3. Cut the feet from the lid; glue to body and let dry.

    4. Cut the wings from the side of egg cups; glue in place and let dry.

    5. Cut the beak from two small pieces of styrofoam. Color this black with felt pen, then glue in place and let dry.

    6. Cut the tail from the peaked portions of the lid; cut to fit the body; glue in place and let dry.

    7. Put a red feather on top of head; draw in the eyes with a black felt pen.

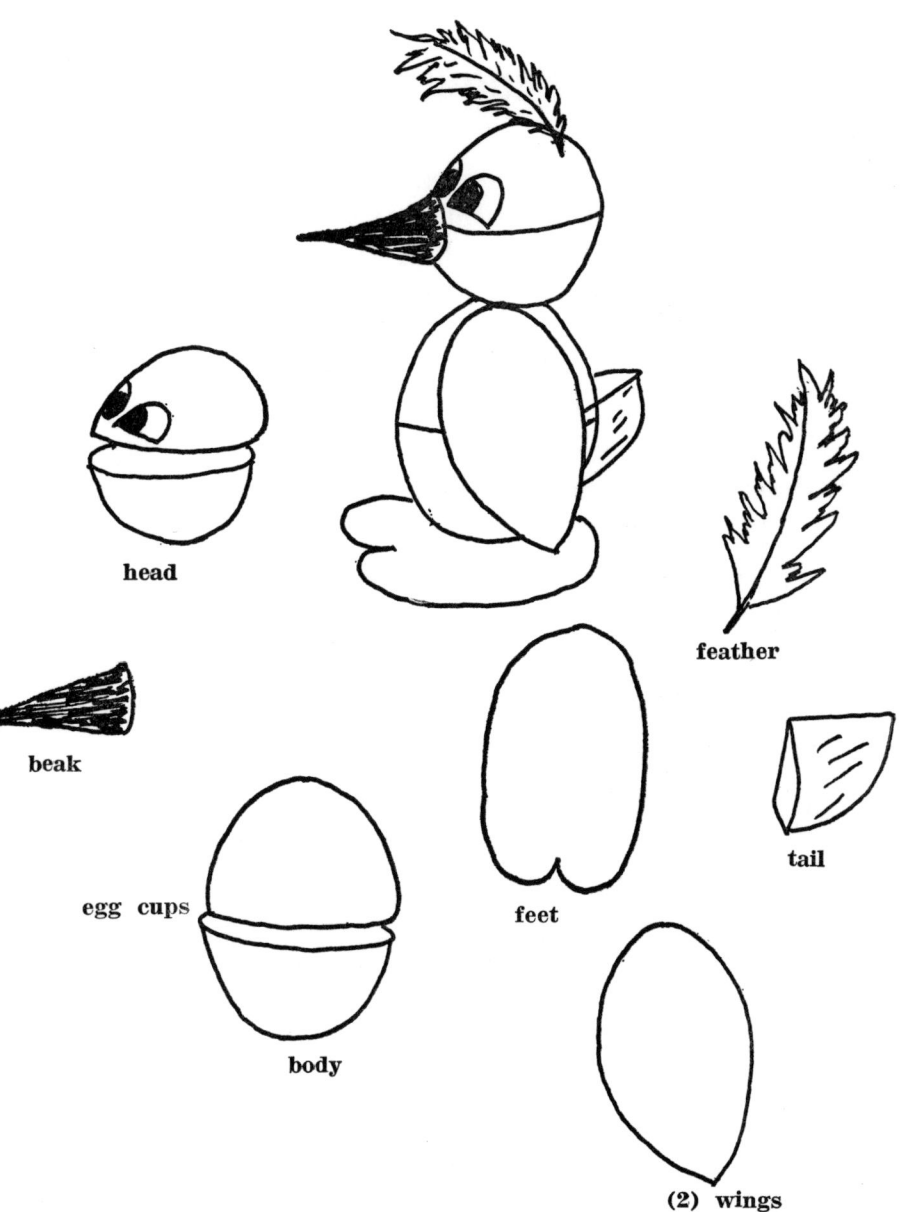

Penguin

Materials needed: 4 egg cups from a white egg carton; the lid of the carton for the base; 2 sides of an egg cup for the wings; 1 of the peaked portions of the lid to make the tail and feet; 2 small pieces to make the beak; 2 small flat beads for the eyes; black felt pen; straight pins

    1. Cut two of the egg cups and make them as large as possible; this will form the body. Cut two of the egg cups smaller; this will form the head. Glue the cups together, then pin and let dry.

    2. Color the head with the black felt pen; also half of the body. Then glue the head and body together and let them dry.

    3. Cut the base from the lid of the carton; glue to body and let dry.

    4. Cut the wings from the side of an egg cup. Color the back of the wing with a black felt pen and glue to each side of the body and let dry.

    5. Cut one of the peaked portions in half for the tail and the feet; color with a black felt pen and glue in place and let dry.

6. Cut two small pieces of styrofoam to make the beak. Color this black with felt pen and glue in place and let dry.

7. Glue and pin small flat beads to the side of the head for the eyes and let dry.

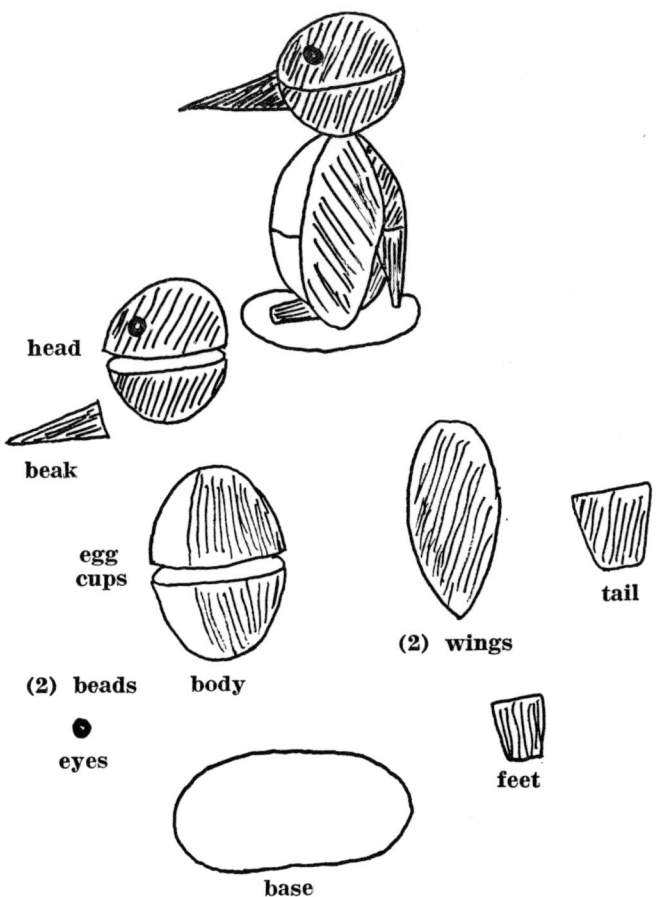

Owl

Materials needed: 4 egg cups from a white egg carton; 2 bottoms of 2 egg cups for the eyes; 2 sides of an egg cup for the wings; 3 triangular pieces for the ears and beaks; brown and black felt pens; straight pins

1. Cut two of the egg cups and make them as large as possible; this will form the body. Cut two of the egg cups smaller; this will form the head. Glue the cups together, then pin to dry.

2. Color the head and body with a brown felt pen. Glue the head and body together and let dry.

3. Cut the wings from the sides of a cup; color with brown felt pen, glue and pin in place, then let dry.

4. Cut the bottom of two egg cups and color the inside with a black felt pen for the eyes. Glue these into place and let dry.

5. Cut two triangular pieces for the ears and color with a brown felt pen; glue and pin into place and let dry.

6. Cut one triangular piece for the beak and color it black with a felt pen; glue and pin into place and let dry.

(2) egg
cup bottoms

eyes

(2) ears

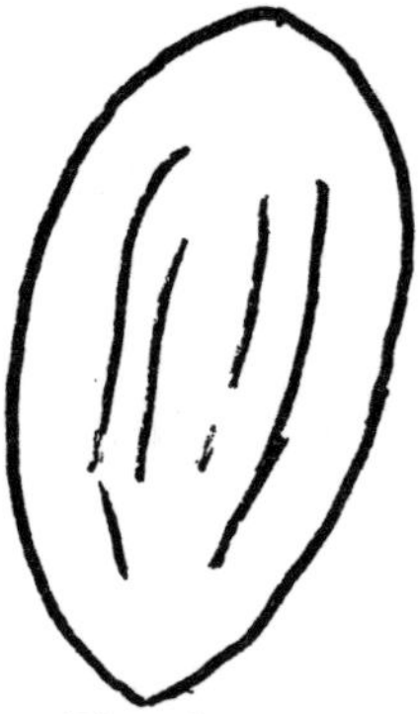

(2) wings

head

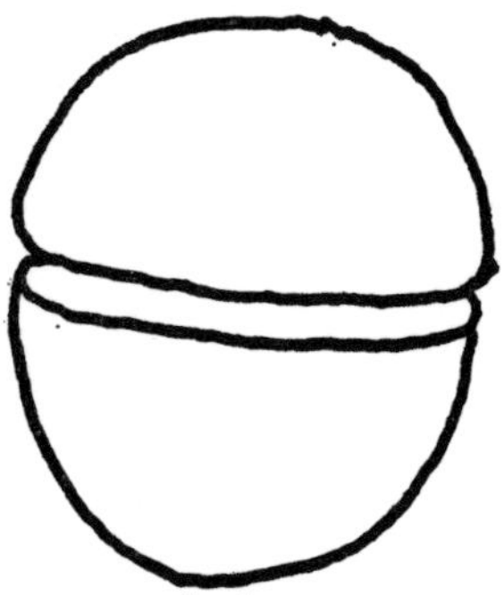

egg cups

beak

body

Swan

Materials needed: 4 egg cups from a white egg carton; 2 peaked fasteners from the lid; 2 beads for the eyes; 1 piece of white pipe cleaner three inches long; 2 small pieces of styrofoam; orange felt pen; straight pins

1. Cut an egg cup, leaving a lip for the tail. Cut another egg cup to make the top of the body. Glue these together; pin and let dry.

2. Cut the two peaked fasteners from the lid of the carton and glue together to make the head.

3. Form an "S" shape out of the pipe cleaner and attach to the body and head by pushing into the styrofoam.

4. Cut wings from the side of an egg cup. Glue these to the sides of the body; pin and let dry.

5. Glue beads to the head for eyes and let dry.

6. Cut two small pieces of styrofoam to make the beak and color with orange felt pen; glue to the head and let dry.

7. Cut base from lid of egg carton and glue swan in place.

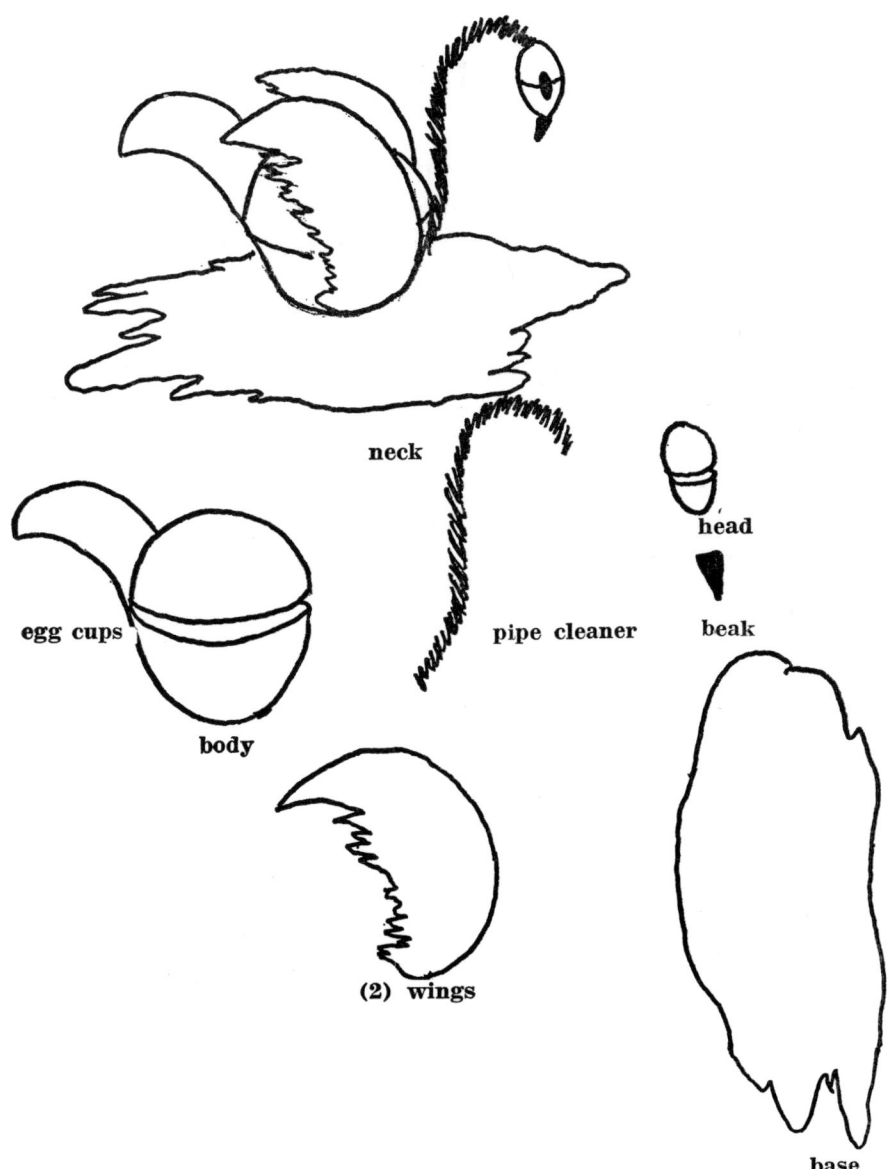

Turkey

Materials needed: 4 egg cups from a white egg carton; 2 peaked fasteners from the lid; 2 beads for the eyes; 1 piece of white pipe cleaner three inches long; 2 small pieces of styrofoam; black felt pen; straight pins

1. Cut an egg cup, leaving a lip for the tail. Cut another egg cup to make the top of the body. Glue these together; pin and let dry.

2. Cut the two peaked fasteners from the lid of the carton and glue together to make the head.

3. Form an "S" shape out of the pipe cleaner and attach to the body and head by pushing into the styrofoam.

4. Cut wings from the side of an egg cup. Glue these to the sides of the body; pin and let dry.

5. Glue beads to the head for eyes and let dry.

6. Cut two small pieces of styrofoam to make the beak and color with a black felt pen; glue to the head and let dry.

7. Can use beard and wattles if desired.

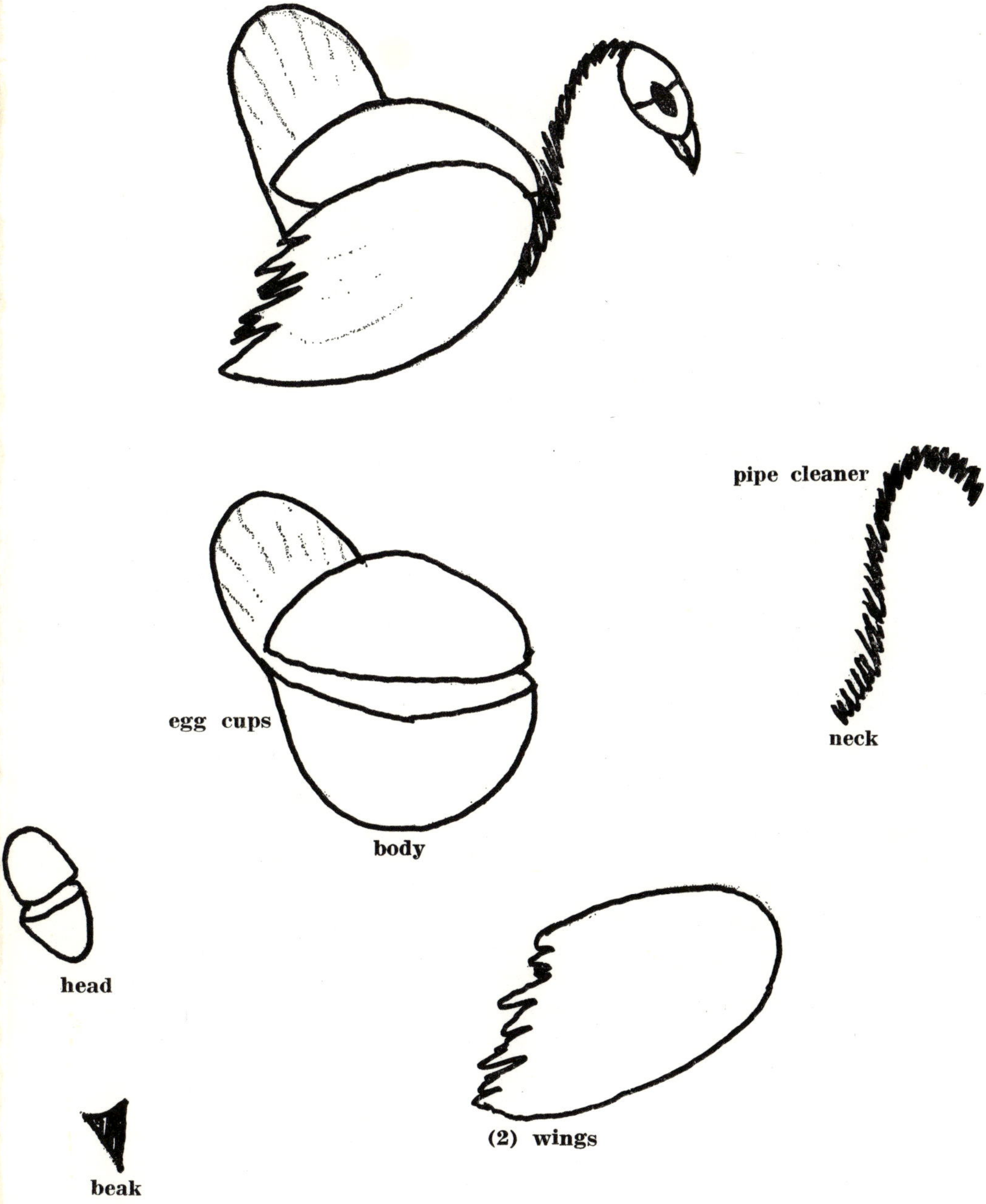

pipe cleaner

egg cups

neck

body

head

beak

(2) wings

Flamingo

Materials needed: 4 egg cups from a pink egg carton; 2 peaked fasteners from the lid; 2 beads for the eyes; 3 pieces of orange pipe cleaner, three inches long; 2 small pieces of styrofoam; black felt pen; straight pins; 1 piece of the lid for base

1. Cut an egg cup, leaving a lip for the tail. Cut another egg cup to make the bottom of the body. Glue these together; pin and let dry.

2. Cut the two peaked fasteners from the lid of the carton and glue together to make the head.

3. Form an "S" shape out of the pipe cleaner and attach to the body and head by pushing into the styrofoam.

4. Cut wings from the side of an egg cup. Glue these to the sides of the body; pin and let dry.

5. Glue beads to the head for eyes and let dry.

6. Cut two small pieces of styrofoam to make the beak and color with a black felt pen; glue to the head and let dry. Cut base from lid.

7. Form the legs out of the pipe cleaners and attach to the body and base by pushing them into the styrofoam.

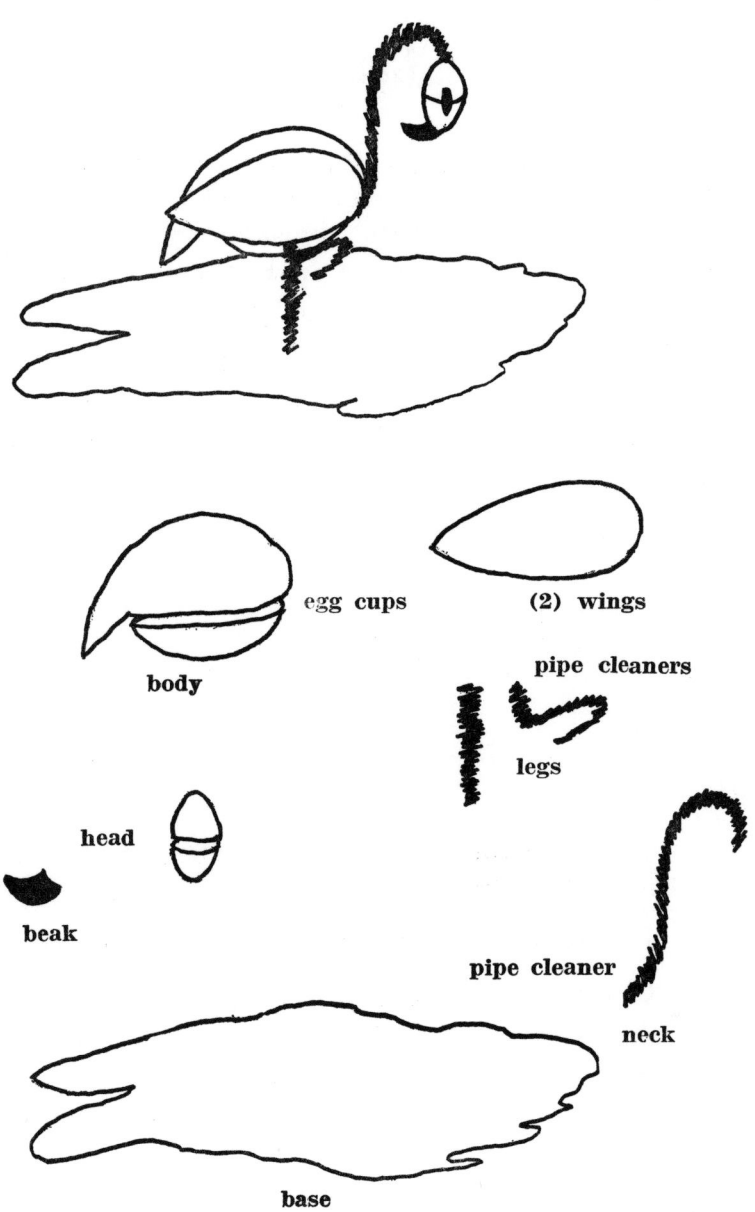

Cat

Materials needed: 4 egg cups from a white egg carton; 1 peaked fastener from the lid for the nose; some broom straws for the whiskers; pipe cleaners for the arms and tail; pieces from the lid to make the ears and feet; black felt pen; straight pins

1. Cut two egg cups and make them as large as possible; this will form the body. Cut two of the egg cups smaller; this will form the head. Glue the cups together, then pin to dry.

2. Glue the head and body together and let them dry.

3. Cut the feet from the lid; glue and let dry.

4. Cut one peaked fastener from the lid, glue it on the head for the nose.

5. Put on the pipe cleaners for the arms and tail.

6. Cut two small triangular pieces for the ears and glue on the head.

7. Put in the broom straws for the whiskers.

8. Color the eyes and mouth with felt pen.

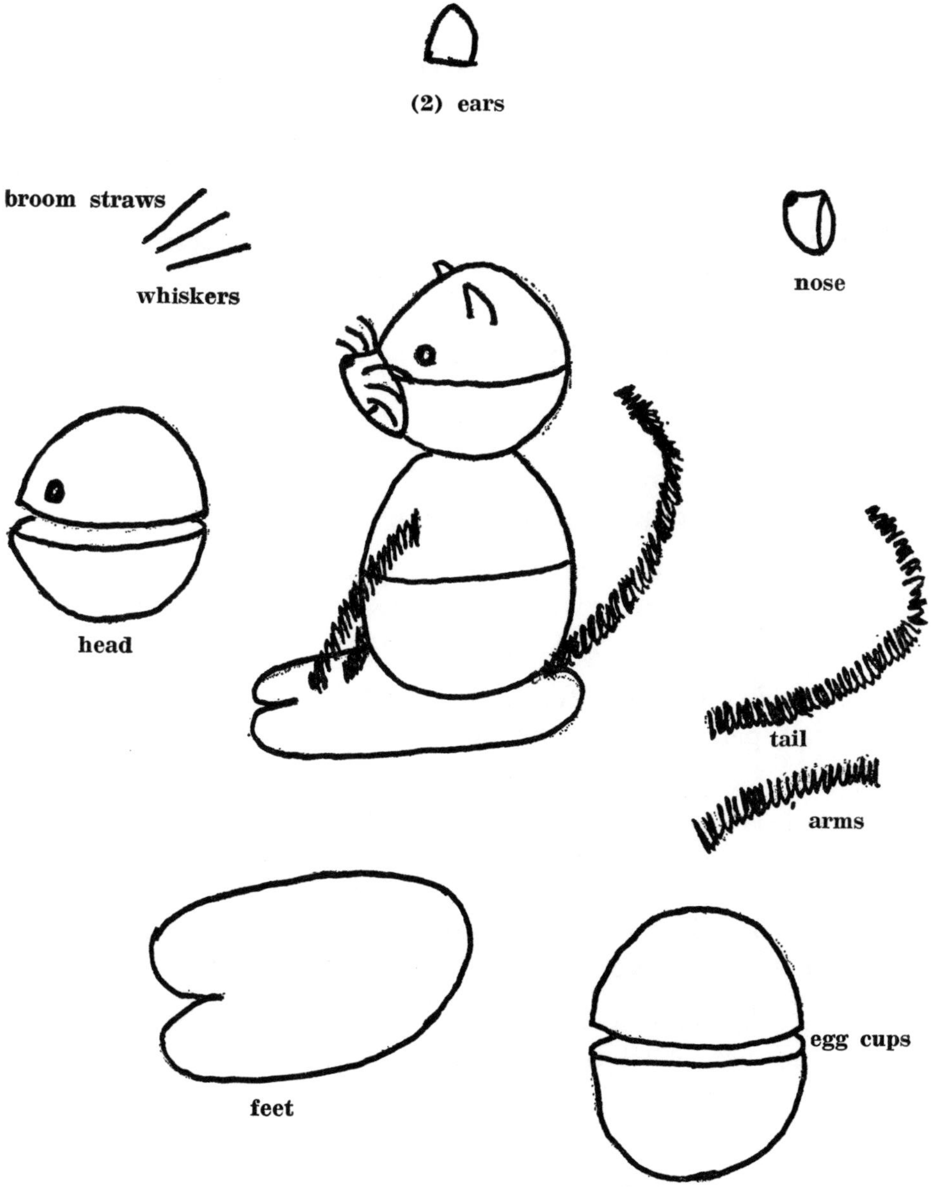

(2) ears

broom straws
whiskers

nose

head

tail

arms

feet

egg cups

body

Squirrel

Materials needed: 4 egg cups from a white egg carton; 1 peaked fastener from the lid for the nose; pipe cleaners for the arms; 2 triangular pieces for the ears from an egg cup; 2 pieces from the lid to make the base and tail; brown and black felt pens; beads for eyes; straight pins

1. Cut two cups and make them as large as possible; this will form the body. Cut two of the egg cups smaller; this will form the head. Glue the cups together, then pin to dry.

2. Color the balls that you have made for the head and body with the brown felt pen, then glue them together and let them dry.

3. Cut the feet from the lid; color with brown felt pen; glue to the body and let dry.

4. Cut one peaked fastener and color it brown before you glue it on the head for the nose.

5. Put pipe cleaners on for the arms.

6. Cut the tail from the side of the lid so that there is a curve. Color it brown and glue it into place.

7. Use a black felt pen to color the mouth and use small beads for the eyes.

8. Cut two small triangular pieces for the ears; round off the top and color them before gluing them on the head.

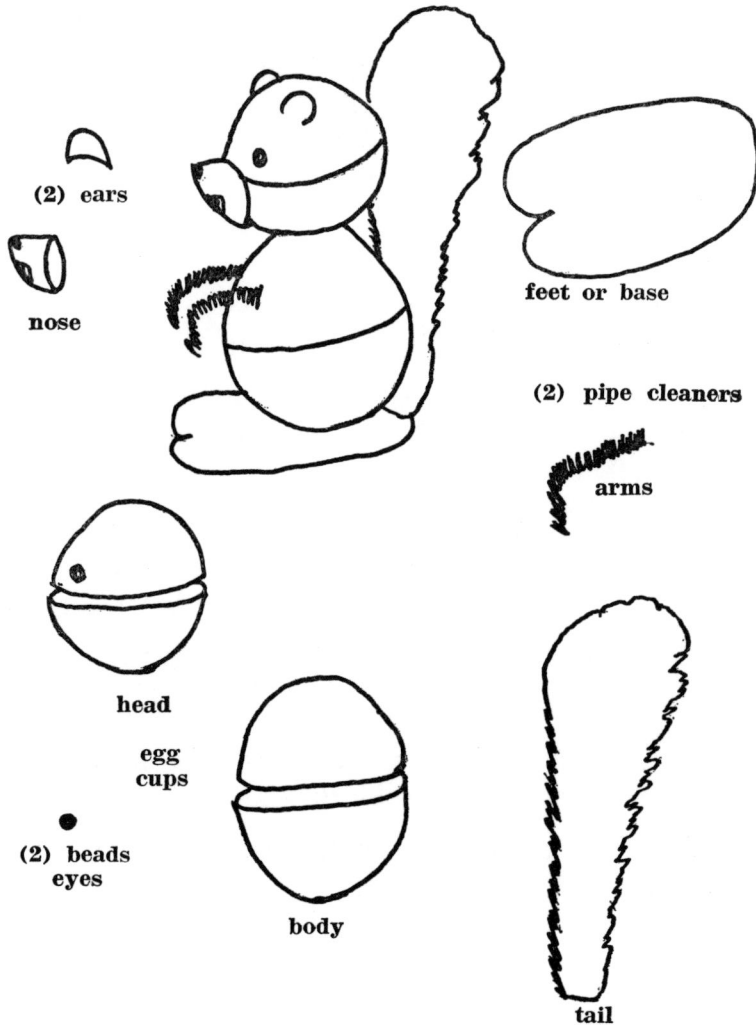

Skunk

Materials needed: 4 egg cups from a white egg carton; 1 peaked fastener from the lid for the nose; pipe cleaners for the arms; 2 triangular pieces for the ears from an egg cup; 2 pieces from the lid to make the base and tail; black felt pen; beads for eyes; 6 broom straws for the whiskers; straight pins

1. Cut two cups and make them as large as possible; this will form the body. Cut two of the egg cups smaller; this will form the head. Glue the cups together, then pin to dry.

2. Color the balls that you have made for the head and body with the black felt pen, then glue them together and let them dry.

3. Cut the feet from the lid; color with black felt pen; glue to the body and let dry.

4. Cut one peaked fastener and color it black before you glue it on the head for the nose.

5. Put on the pipe cleaners for the arms.

6. Cut the tail from the side of the lid so that there is a curve. Color it black and glue in place.

7. Use a black felt pen to color the mouth and use small beads for the eyes.

8. Cut two small triangular pieces for the ears;

round off the top and color them before gluing them on the head.

9. Put in broom straws for whiskers.

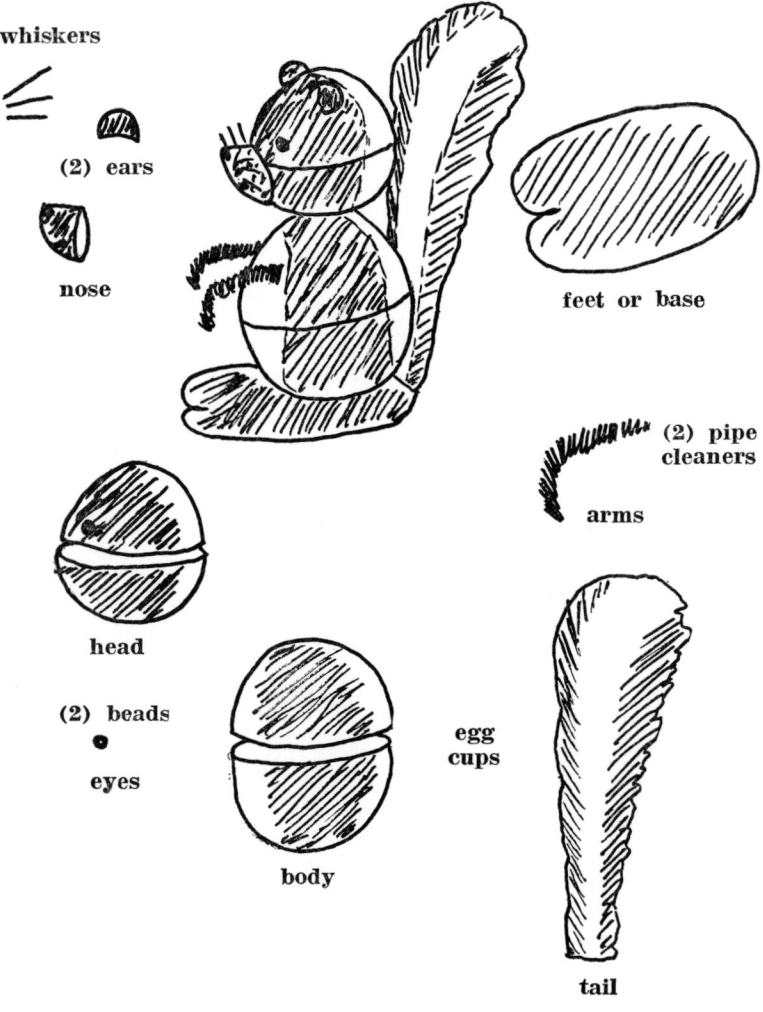

Raccoon

Materials needed: 4 egg cups from a white egg carton; 1 peaked fastener from the lid, for the nose; yellow pipe cleaners for the arms and tail; 2 triangular pieces for the ears from an egg cup; 1 piece from the lid to make the base; brown and black felt pens; beads for the eyes; straight pins

1. Cut two cups and make them as large as possible; this will form the body. Cut two of the egg cups smaller; this will form the head. Glue the cups together, then pin to dry.

2. Color the balls that you have made for the head and body with the brown felt pen, then glue them together and let them dry.

3. Cut the feet from the lid; color with brown felt pen; glue to the body and let dry.

4. Cut one peaked fastener and color it brown before you glue it on the head for the nose.

5. Put on the pipe cleaners for the arms and tail.

6. Use a black felt pen to color a mask around the eyes, and to make black rings on the yellow pipe cleaner tail.

7. Put on beads for the eyes.

8. Cut two small triangular pieces for the ears; round off the top and color them before gluing them on the head.

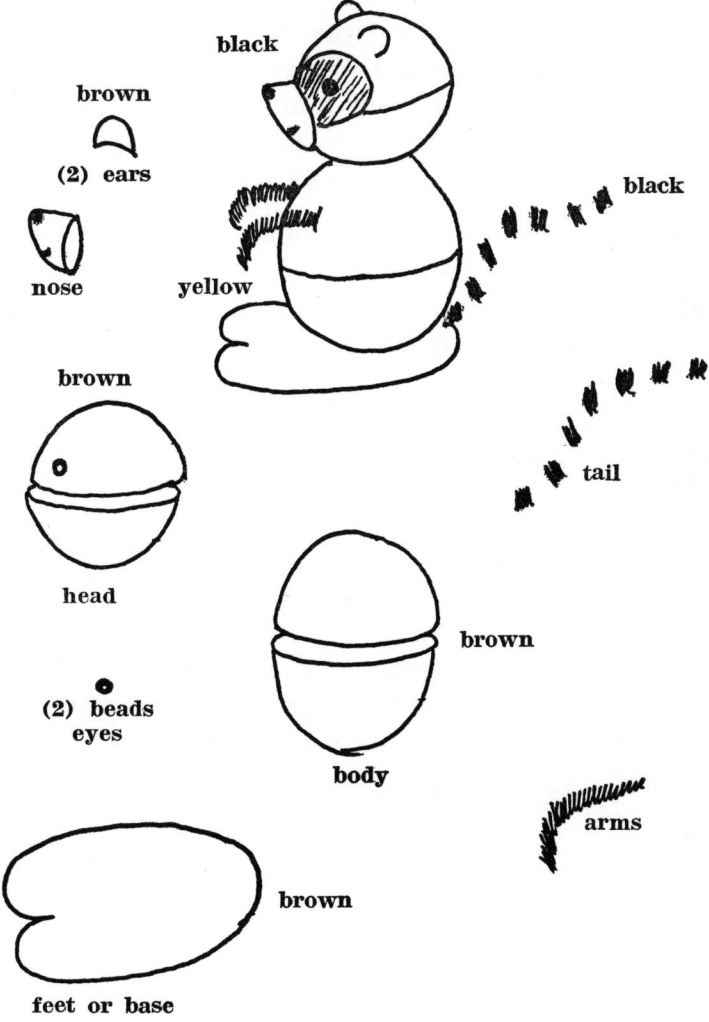

Rabbit

Materials needed: 4 egg cups from a white egg carton; 1 peaked fastener from the lid, for the nose; white pipe cleaners for the arms; 3 pieces from the lid for the ears and feet; black and red felt pens; beads for the eyes; 6 broom straws for the whiskers; a piece of cotton for the tail; straight pins

1. Cut two cups and make them as large as possible; this will form the body. Cut two of the egg cups smaller; this will form the head. Glue the cups together, then pin to dry.

2. Glue the two balls together and let them dry.

3. Cut the feet from the lid; glue to the body and let dry.

4. Cut one peaked fastener for the nose and color it light red with black markings, then glue it on the head.

5. Cut the two ears from the lid and color the inside light red. Then slash small slits in the top of the head on either side and push ears in slits.

6. Make the mouth on nose portion with black pen.

7. Put on pipe cleaners for the arms, and glue cotton on for tail; beads for the eyes; broom straws for the whiskers.

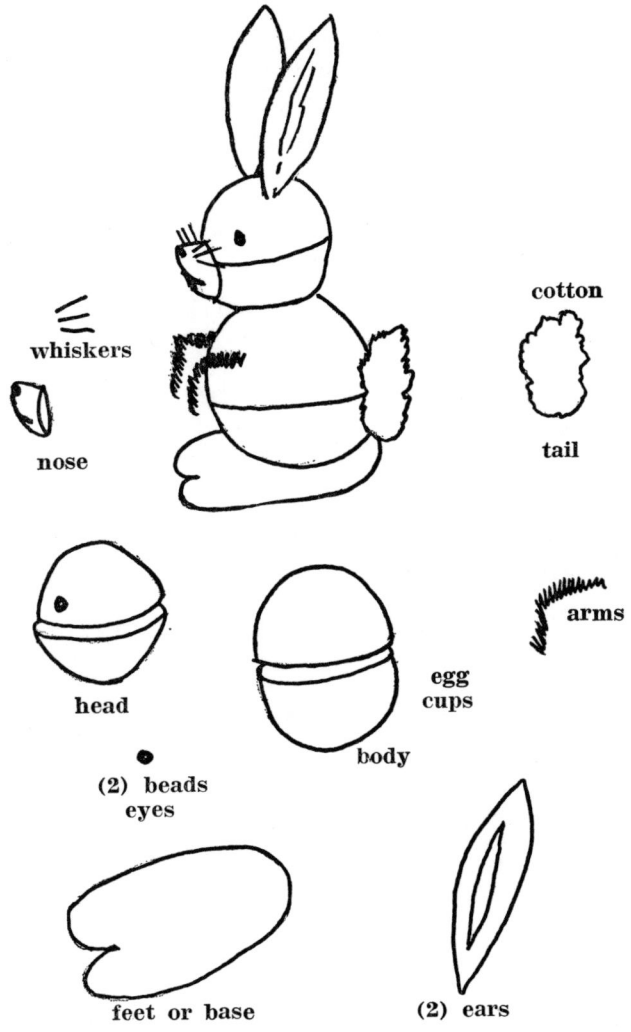

Mouse

Materials needed: 4 egg cups from a white egg carton; 1 peaked fastener from the lid for the nose; white pipe cleaners for the arms, ears, and tail; 1 piece from the lid for the feet; black and red felt pens; beads for the eyes; 6 broom straws for the whiskers; straight pins

1. Cut two cups and make them as large as possible; this will form the body. Cut two of the egg cups smaller; this will form the head. Glue the cups together, then pin to dry.

2. Glue the two balls together and let them dry.

3. Cut the feet from the lid; glue to the body and let dry.

4. Cut one peaked fastener for the nose and color it with the pens before you glue it on the head.

5. Put on the pipe cleaners for the arms, ears and tail.

6. Color the mouth on the nose portion.

7. Put on beads for the eyes.

8. Put in broom straws for the whiskers.

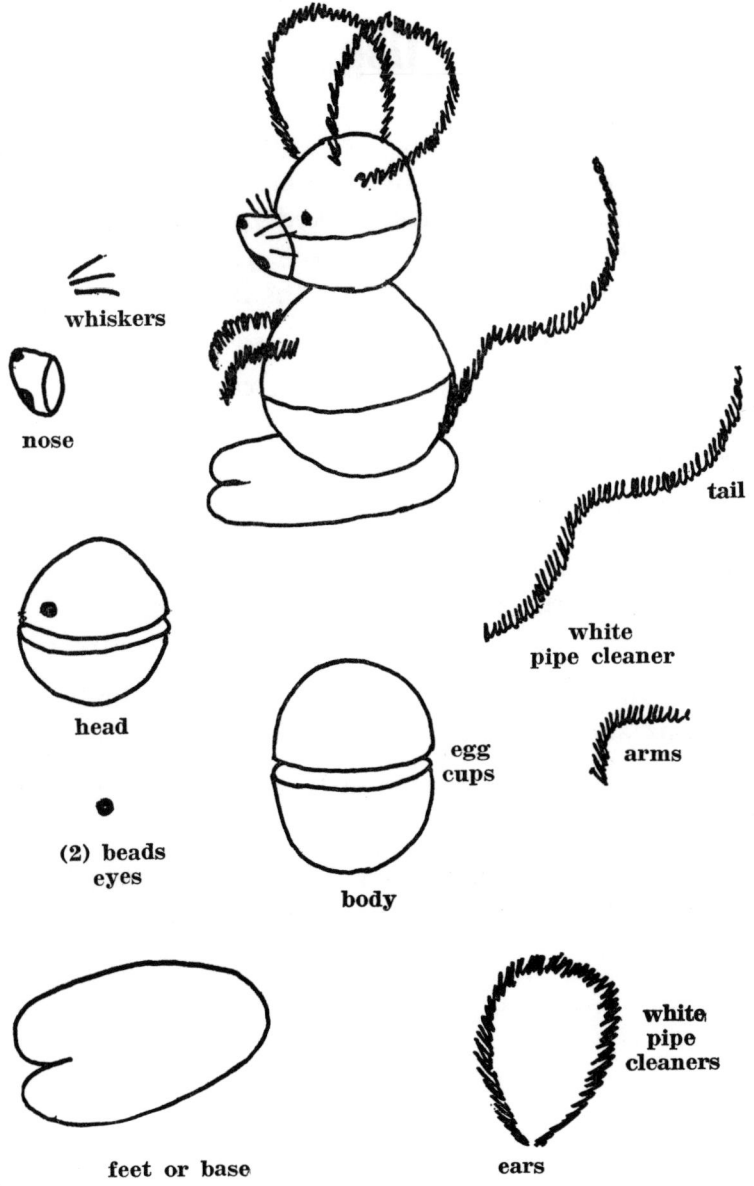

Dog

Materials needed: 4 egg cups any desired color; black felt pen; 3 pieces of pipe cleaner any color for the tail and legs; 2 of the peaked parts of the carton between the egg cups for the nose, the crown and the ears; flat portions of the lid for the base; straight pins

1. Cut two egg cups and make them as large as possible to make the body. Then cut two more egg cups a little smaller to make the head; glue and pin together and let dry.

2. Cut a peaked part between the egg cups to fit the head; glue and let dry to make the nose.

3. Glue the head and body to the base and let dry.

4. Stick the pipe cleaners into the body for the arms and the tail.

5. Color the nose, mouth and eyes with black felt pen.

6. Cut a peaked part between the egg cups, leaving a lip on two sides, to make the ears; glue to the head.

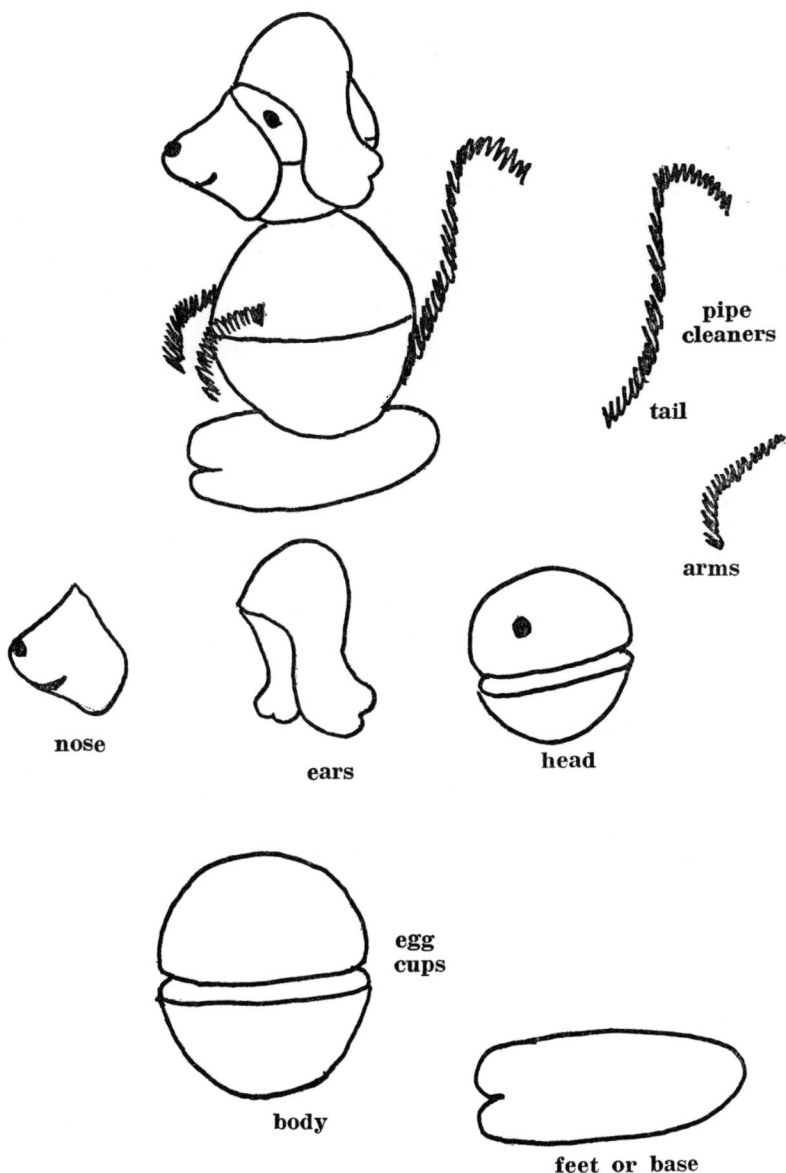

Frog

Materials needed: 4 egg cups from a green egg carton; one peaked part between the egg cups; a small flat piece of the lid for the base; 4 pieces of green pipe cleaner three inches long; 2 lid fasteners for the eyes; straight pins; black felt pen

    1. Cut two egg cups and make them as large as possible to make the body. Then cut two more egg cups a little smaller to make the head; glue and pin together and let dry.

    2. Cut a peaked part between the egg cups; this will make the nose; glue to head; pin and let dry.

    3. Cut the lid fasteners and glue to the head to make the eyes. Color the end of the fasteners for the eyes.

    4. Glue the head and body to the base and let dry.

    5. Stick the green pipe cleaners into the body for the arms and legs; bend to the shape wanted.

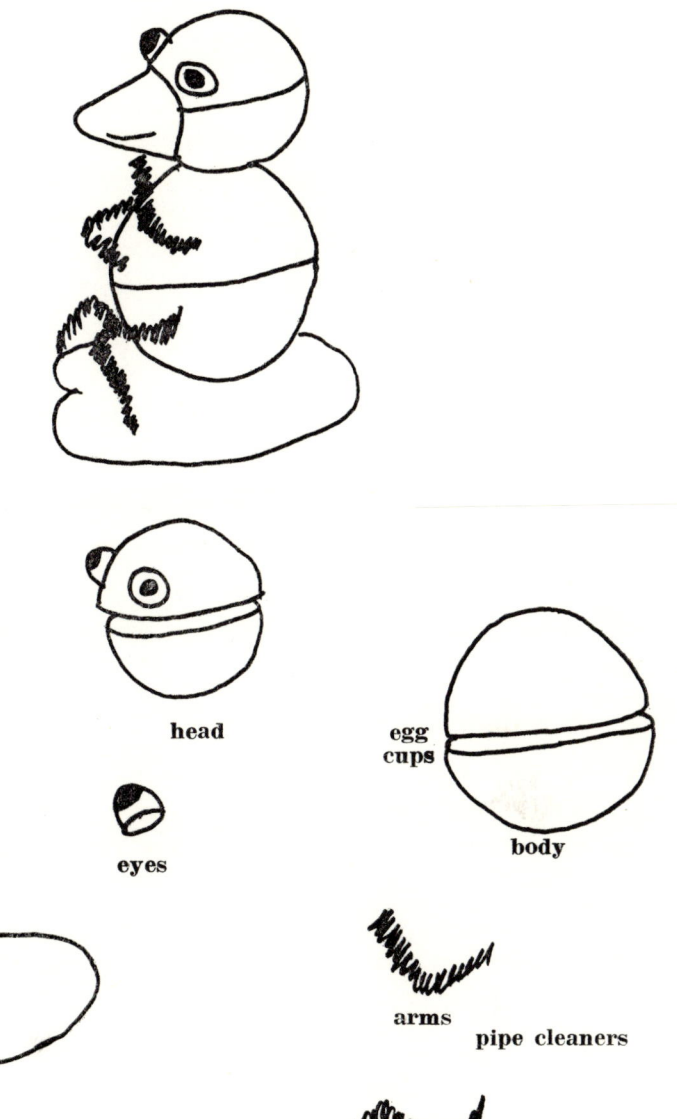

WITHDRAWN